The Garden Buddies Party

Twilight to Dusk

Margaret Kamla Kumar
Laila Savolainen

Copyright © 2023
The moral right of Margaret Kamla Kumar to be identified as the Author and Laila Savolainen as the Illustrator of the work has been asserted by them in accordance with the Copyright, Designs and Patents Act 1988.

All rights reserved. No part of this book may be used or reproduced, stored in a retrieval system, or transmitted in any form, or by any means electronic, mechanical, recording, photocopying, or in any manner whatsoever without permission in writing from the publisher, except for the inclusion of brief quotations in a review.

A catalogue record for this book is available from the National Library of Australia

ISBN: 978-0-6458192-5-0 (paperback)
ISBN: 978-0-6458192-7-4 (hardback)
ISBN: 978-0-6458192-6-7 (e-book)

This book is part of the: Kashy Koala Series - Environmentally Aware
Author: Margaret Kamla Kumar
Illustrator: Laila Savolainen

Interior / Cover / Artwork: Pickawoowoo Author Services
Print and Channel Distribution: Lightning Source / Ingram (US/UK/AUS/EUR)

Publisher: Uma Publishing Group
www.umapublishing.com

Dedication

This book is dedicated to the joy of participation and community spirit.

It is an in-between time in this part of the world.

This time is referred to as the evening twilight.

The garden is half in shadow and half in light.

The trees look like friendly shadows.

The sun is moving below the horizon.

Stars are beginning to appear as tiny points of light.

The setting sun makes the sky neither light nor dark.

It is not dusk.

It is the perfect time for the Garden Buddies, to hold a party.

They choose to hold the party inside a water fountain.

There is no water in the fountain because of the dry season.

The water fountain stands on a cemented stool that is shaped like a boot. The boot is red in colour. It is decorated with black soil to help it stand.

Green moss, algae and shiny green leaves wrap around the red boot.

The evening twilight gives the water fountain rays of golden light.

The water fountain appears and disappears in the evening twilight.

It is party time for the Garden Buddies. The party begins.

The grasshopper stands on the edge of the fountain.

It is like a lighthouse guiding the Garden Buddies to the party.

The Dusk hawker dragonfly breezes in. "I know I am necessary at this party. The evening twilight and dusk are my home," it says.

Not to be outdone, the cicadas arrive to show their skills. Their wings begin to produce a buzzing noise. Bzzzzzzzzzzz. It seems as if they will burst into a song any minute.

A pair of crickets arrive with a chirping musical sound.

Their wings work at such a fast pace that it seems as if they are making one long musical note that will never end.

The Spiny Leaf Insects often called experts in disguise swoop into the centre of the fountain. They look like unique origami or dead gum leaves with wings attached. Their arrival at the party is announced with clicking noises.

Other friends begin to arrive. The frilled lizard jumps down from a tree branch into the fountain. It elegantly spreads out its frilled collar and swirls it in the evening twilight breeze.

Not wanting to draw attention, the ladybirds shuffle in very quietly.

Their shells give off spectacular colours that light up the fountain.

A swarm of tropical butterflies come in fluttering their wings.

They duck and swirl above the water fountain.

"No water?" They wonder what is happening in the water fountain.

Another friend that arrives is the little green frog. It takes a giant leap from a red cabbage leaf and lands on the shoelaces of the red boot.

It somersaults up to the water fountain.

"Croak croak! did you think I would forget?" it says to the grasshopper.

Joey Koalakin watching from a eucalyptus tree above wonders what they are all doing.

"I must ask Mama and Grandfather," he says. "Maybe I can join them."

He clambers down to the branch where Mama Akashi and Grandfather Kashy are waiting for him before they all go searching for gum leaves. Joey Koalakin tells them what he just saw.

They look across to the Garden Buddies Party and then Grandfather Kashy says, "That is a new story, little Koalakin for another time. Our friends are enjoying themselves before dusk settles in."

Dusk begins to settle in.

The colours of the evening twilight begin to disappear.

The sun disappears beneath the horizon.

The golden rays on the red boot stand change to silver lines.

They show the way for the many stars that light up the galaxy.

Dusk turns into night-time.

A full moon appears.

It comes on top of the Garden Buddies.

The Garden Buddies seeing this know that it is time to leave the party.

They say goodbye to each other, promising to return to another fun-filled evening twilight party.

Titles Available

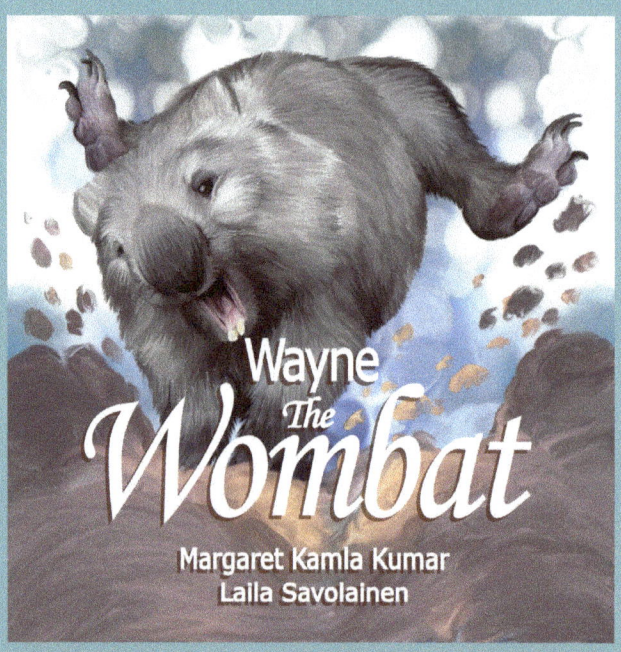
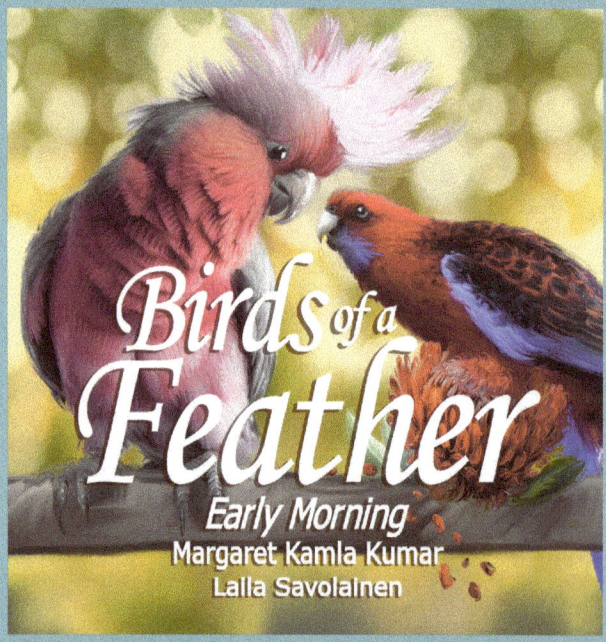

www.ingramcontent.com/pod-product-compliance
Lightning Source LLC
Chambersburg PA
CBHW040728020526
44107CB00085B/2960